MW01029711

TODAY

I MANIFEST & CREATE THE LIFE I DESIRE

This 55x5 Challenge Workbook Belongs to:

Copyright © 2019 555 Challenge: The Law of Attraction Writing Exercise Journal & Workbook to for Women to Manifest Your Desires with the 55x5 Manifestation Technique

All rights reserved. No part of this book may be reproduced in any form or by any electronic or mechanical means, including information storage and retrieval systems, without permission in writing from the publisher, except by reviewers, who may quote brief passages in a review.

Make it Happen Publishing Inc.

www.mihpublishing.com
Send all inquires to books@mihpublishing.com

THE LAW OF ATTRACTION TECHNIQUE: 55X5 CHALLENGE

WHAT TO DO:

Focus on one goal and write out a clear statement in the present tense (like you already have it and from a place of gratitude) that outlines what you desire. For 5 consecutive days you will write out this statement 55 times. Be sure to stay focused while you're writing your lines and be sure to complete all 55 lines during your daily session. At the end of the 5th day, release your intention and trust that it will come!

(For example: "I am excited and thankful for the extra $10,000 in my bank account this month")

55X5 MANIFESTING CHALLENGE TIPS

- Use a Pen! Purple, blue or red are preferred.

- Prepare by getting into a relaxed state/mood. Ambient light or candles, soothing music etc.

- Remove any possible distractions and be mindful and present when writing your lines.

- Be clear and detailed about what you want to manifest. Keep it to one sentence.

- Including words of gratitude and emotions into your statement are essential!

- Be excited about what you are manifesting - Feel the emotions of receiving what you want.

- Work on only one goal at a time (for the consecutive 5 days) before moving to the next one.

- This is not homework and it should not feel bad to do. Get into a high vibrational space.

- Saying the words as you write them can help keep you focused.

- Visualize your life as you want it to be.

- Meditating before and after writing your daily lines is beneficial.

- DO NOT SKIP A DAY or SPLIT YOUR 55 LINES INTO DIFFERENT TIMES DURING THE DAY

- ALL 55 LINES MUST BE WRITTEN DURING ONE SESSION.

- At the end of 5 days - release your affirmation and trust that the Universe will bring it to you.

- When you've completed the 55X5 Challenge and have successfully manifested your goal, remember to record your success in this journal for future reference and confirmation.

- Be grateful for all that the Universe brings to you!

*** *NOW GO AND GET STARTED ON MANIFESTING THE LIFE YOU WANT AND DESERVE!* ***

MANIFESTATION INTENTION:

(In the present tense & a place of gratitude, write a clear statement of your intended manifestation as if you already have it)

1
2
3
4
5
6
7
8
9
10
11
12
13
14
15
16
17
18
19
20
21
22
23
24
25

26

27

28

29

30

31

32

33

34

35

36

37

38

39

40

41

42

43

44

45

46

47

48

49

50

51

52

53

54

55

I RELEASE MY INTENTION WITH GRATITUDE AND LOVE,

MANIFESTATION MINDSET: Why do you desire this intention in your life?

(Get into the right mindset before you continue to write out the EXACT SAME manifestation intention from day 1 below)

1
2
3
4
5
6
7
8
9
10
11
12
13
14
15
16
17
18
19
20
21
22
23
24
25

26

27

28

29

30

31

32

33

34

35

36

37

38

39

40

41

42

43

44

45

46

47

48

49

50

51

52

53

54

55

I RELEASE MY INTENTION WITH GRATITUDE AND LOVE,

MANIFESTATION MINDSET: Why does this intention excite you?

(Get into the right mindset before you continue to write out the EXACT SAME manifestation intention from day 1 below)

1

2

3

4

5

6

7

8

9

10

11

12

13

14

15

16

17

18

19

20

21

22

23

24

25

26
27
28
29
30
31
32
33
34
35
36
37
38
39
40
41
42
43
44
45
46
47
48
49
50
51
52
53
54
55

I RELEASE MY INTENTION WITH GRATITUDE AND LOVE,

MANIFESTATION MINDSET: How is your life better because of this intention?

(Get into the right mindset before you continue to write out the EXACT SAME manifestation intention from day 1 below)

1
2
3
4
5
6
7
8
9
10
11
12
13
14
15
16
17
18
19
20
21
22
23
24
25

26

27

28

29

30

31

32

33

34

35

36

37

38

39

40

41

42

43

44

45

46

47

48

49

50

51

52

53

54

55

I RELEASE MY INTENTION WITH GRATITUDE AND LOVE,

MANIFESTATION MINDSET: Why are you grateful to have this intention?

(Get into the right mindset before you continue to write out the EXACT SAME manifestation intention from day 1 below)

1
2
3
4
5
6
7
8
9
10
11
12
13
14
15
16
17
18
19
20
21
22
23
24
25

26
27
28
29
30
31
32
33
34
35
36
37
38
39
40
41
42
43
44
45
46
47
48
49
50
51
52
53
54
55

I RELEASE MY INTENTION WITH GRATITUDE AND LOVE,

55X5 CHALLENGE COMPLETED ON DATE ____/____/____ TIME ____:____ AM / PM

MANIFESTED INTENTION:

(REWRITE THE EXACT SAME manifestation intention from day 1 above)

MANIFESTATION SUCCESS STORY

Use these pages to write, illustrate or attach photos, receipts, evidence or proof of your 55x5 Success Story. This will help to document your manifesting journey and minimize resistence to future manifestations and the Law of Attraction.

55X5 CHALLENGE COMPLETION

55X5 CHALLENGE COMPLETION

MANIFESTATION INTENTION:

(In the present tense & a place of gratitude, write a clear statement of your intended manifestation as if you already have it)

1

2

3

4

5

6

7

8

9

10

11

12

13

14

15

16

17

18

19

20

21

22

23

24

25

DAY 1

26
27
28
29
30
31
32
33
34
35
36
37
38
39
40
41
42
43
44
45
46
47
48
49
50
51
52
53
54
55

I RELEASE MY INTENTION WITH GRATITUDE AND LOVE,

MANIFESTATION MINDSET: Why do you desire this intention in your life?

(Get into the right mindset before you continue to write out the EXACT SAME manifestation intention from day 1 below)

1

2

3

4

5

6

7

8

9

10

11

12

13

14

15

16

17

18

19

20

21

22

23

24

25

26
27
28
29
30
31
32
33
34
35
36
37
38
39
40
41
42
43
44
45
46
47
48
49
50
51
52
53
54
55

I RELEASE MY INTENTION WITH GRATITUDE AND LOVE,

MANIFESTATION MINDSET: Why does this intention excite you?

(Get into the right mindset before you continue to write out the EXACT SAME manifestation intention from day 1 below)

1

2

3

4

5

6

7

8

9

10

11

12

13

14

15

16

17

18

19

20

21

22

23

24

25

26

27

28

29

30

31

32

33

34

35

36

37

38

39

40

41

42

43

44

45

46

47

48

49

50

51

52

53

54

55

I RELEASE MY INTENTION WITH GRATITUDE AND LOVE,

MANIFESTATION MINDSET: How is your life better because of this intention?

(Get into the right mindset before you continue to write out the EXACT SAME manifestation intention from day 1 below)

1
2
3
4
5
6
7
8
9
10
11
12
13
14
15
16
17
18
19
20
21
22
23
24
25

26
27
28
29
30
31
32
33
34
35
36
37
38
39
40
41
42
43
44
45
46
47
48
49
50
51
52
53
54
55

I RELEASE MY INTENTION WITH GRATITUDE AND LOVE,

MANIFESTATION MINDSET: Why are you grateful to have this intention?

(Get into the right mindset before you continue to write out the EXACT SAME manifestation intention from day 1 below)

1

2

3

4

5

6

7

8

9

10

11

12

13

14

15

16

17

18

19

20

21

22

23

24

25

DAY 5

26

27

28

29

30

31

32

33

34

35

36

37

38

39

40

41

42

43

44

45

46

47

48

49

50

51

52

53

54

55

I RELEASE MY INTENTION WITH GRATITUDE AND LOVE,

MANIFESTED INTENTION:

(REWRITE THE EXACT SAME manifestation intention from day 1 above)

MANIFESTATION SUCCESS STORY

Use these pages to write, illustrate or attach photos, receipts, evidence or proof of your 55x5 Success Story. This will help to document your manifesting journey and minimize resistence to future manifestations and the Law of Attraction.

MANIFESTATION INTENTION:

(In the present tense & a place of gratitude, write a clear statement of your intended manifestation as if you already have it)

1

2

3

4

5

6

7

8

9

10

11

12

13

14

15

16

17

18

19

20

21

22

23

24

25

26
27
28
29
30
31
32
33
34
35
36
37
38
39
40
41
42
43
44
45
46
47
48
49
50
51
52
53
54
55

I RELEASE MY INTENTION WITH GRATITUDE AND LOVE,

MANIFESTATION MINDSET: Why do you desire this intention in your life?

(Get into the right mindset before you continue to write out the EXACT SAME manifestation intention from day 1 below)

1

2

3

4

5

6

7

8

9

10

11

12

13

14

15

16

17

18

19

20

21

22

23

24

25

26

27

28

29

30

31

32

33

34

35

36

37

38

39

40

41

42

43

44

45

46

47

48

49

50

51

52

53

54

55

I RELEASE MY INTENTION WITH GRATITUDE AND LOVE,

MANIFESTATION MINDSET: Why does this intention excite you?

(Get into the right mindset before you continue to write out the EXACT SAME manifestation intention from day 1 below)

1

2

3

4

5

6

7

8

9

10

11

12

13

14

15

16

17

18

19

20

21

22

23

24

25

DAY 3

26
27
28
29
30
31
32
33
34
35
36
37
38
39
40
41
42
43
44
45
46
47
48
49
50
51
52
53
54
55

I RELEASE MY INTENTION WITH GRATITUDE AND LOVE,

MANIFESTATION MINDSET: How is your life better because of this intention?

(Get into the right mindset before you continue to write out the EXACT SAME manifestation intention from day 1 below)

1
2
3
4
5
6
7
8
9
10
11
12
13
14
15
16
17
18
19
20
21
22
23
24
25

26

27

28

29

30

31

32

33

34

35

36

37

38

39

40

41

42

43

44

45

46

47

48

49

50

51

52

53

54

55

I RELEASE MY INTENTION WITH GRATITUDE AND LOVE,

MANIFESTATION MINDSET: Why are you grateful to have this intention?

(Get into the right mindset before you continue to write out the EXACT SAME manifestation intention from day 1 below)

1
2
3
4
5
6
7
8
9
10
11
12
13
14
15
16
17
18
19
20
21
22
23
24
25

26

27

28

29

30

31

32

33

34

35

36

37

38

39

40

41

42

43

44

45

46

47

48

49

50

51

52

53

54

55

I RELEASE MY INTENTION WITH GRATITUDE AND LOVE,

MANIFESTED INTENTION:

(REWRITE THE EXACT SAME manifestation intention from day 1 above)

MANIFESTATION SUCCESS STORY

Use these pages to write, illustrate or attach photos, receipts, evidence or proof of your 55x5 Success Story. This will help to document your manifesting journey and minimize resistence to future manifestations and the Law of Attraction.

55X5 CHALLENGE COMPLETION

MANIFESTATION INTENTION:

(In the present tense & a place of gratitude, write a clear statement of your intended manifestation as if you already have it)

1
2
3
4
5
6
7
8
9
10
11
12
13
14
15
16
17
18
19
20
21
22
23
24
25

26

27

28

29

30

31

32

33

34

35

36

37

38

39

40

41

42

43

44

45

46

47

48

49

50

51

52

53

54

55

I RELEASE MY INTENTION WITH GRATITUDE AND LOVE,

MANIFESTATION MINDSET: Why do you desire this intention in your life?

(Get into the right mindset before you continue to write out the EXACT SAME manifestation intention from day 1 below)

1

2

3

4

5

6

7

8

9

10

11

12

13

14

15

16

17

18

19

20

21

22

23

24

25

26
27
28
29
30
31
32
33
34
35
36
37
38
39
40
41
42
43
44
45
46
47
48
49
50
51
52
53
54
55

I RELEASE MY INTENTION WITH GRATITUDE AND LOVE,

MANIFESTATION MINDSET: Why does this intention excite you?

(Get into the right mindset before you continue to write out the EXACT SAME manifestation intention from day 1 below)

1
2
3
4
5
6
7
8
9
10
11
12
13
14
15
16
17
18
19
20
21
22
23
24
25

26
27
28
29
30
31
32
33
34
35
36
37
38
39
40
41
42
43
44
45
46
47
48
49
50
51
52
53
54
55

I RELEASE MY INTENTION WITH GRATITUDE AND LOVE,

MANIFESTATION MINDSET: How is your life better because of this intention?

(Get into the right mindset before you continue to write out the EXACT SAME manifestation intention from day 1 below)

1
2
3
4
5
6
7
8
9
10
11
12
13
14
15
16
17
18
19
20
21
22
23
24
25

26
27
28
29
30
31
32
33
34
35
36
37
38
39
40
41
42
43
44
45
46
47
48
49
50
51
52
53
54
55

I RELEASE MY INTENTION WITH GRATITUDE AND LOVE,

MANIFESTATION MINDSET: Why are you grateful to have this intention?

(Get into the right mindset before you continue to write out the EXACT SAME manifestation intention from day 1 below)

1
2
3
4
5
6
7
8
9
10
11
12
13
14
15
16
17
18
19
20
21
22
23
24
25

26

27

28

29

30

31

32

33

34

35

36

37

38

39

40

41

42

43

44

45

46

47

48

49

50

51

52

53

54

55

I RELEASE MY INTENTION WITH GRATITUDE AND LOVE,

55X5 CHALLENGE COMPLETED ON DATE ____/____/____ TIME ____:____ AM / PM

MANIFESTED INTENTION:

(REWRITE THE EXACT SAME manifestation intention from day 1 above)

MANIFESTATION SUCCESS STORY

Use these pages to write, illustrate or attach photos, receipts, evidence or proof of your 55x5 Success Story. This will help to document your manifesting journey and minimize resistence to future manifestations and the Law of Attraction.

55X5 CHALLENGE COMPLETION

MANIFESTATION INTENTION:

(In the present tense & a place of gratitude, write a clear statement of your intended manifestation as if you already have it)

1
2
3
4
5
6
7
8
9
10
11
12
13
14
15
16
17
18
19
20
21
22
23
24
25

26
27
28
29
30
31
32
33
34
35
36
37
38
39
40
41
42
43
44
45
46
47
48
49
50
51
52
53
54
55

I RELEASE MY INTENTION WITH GRATITUDE AND LOVE,

MANIFESTATION MINDSET: Why do you desire this intention in your life?

(Get into the right mindset before you continue to write out the EXACT SAME manifestation intention from day 1 below)

1

2

3

4

5

6

7

8

9

10

11

12

13

14

15

16

17

18

19

20

21

22

23

24

25

26
27
28
29
30
31
32
33
34
35
36
37
38
39
40
41
42
43
44
45
46
47
48
49
50
51
52
53
54
55

I RELEASE MY INTENTION WITH GRATITUDE AND LOVE,

DATE _____/_____/_____   TIME _____:_____AM / PM

MANIFESTATION MINDSET: Why does this intention excite you?

(Get into the right mindset before you continue to write out the EXACT SAME manifestation intention from day 1 below)

1
2
3
4
5
6
7
8
9
10
11
12
13
14
15
16
17
18
19
20
21
22
23
24
25

26

27

28

29

30

31

32

33

34

35

36

37

38

39

40

41

42

43

44

45

46

47

48

49

50

51

52

53

54

55

I RELEASE MY INTENTION WITH GRATITUDE AND LOVE,

MANIFESTATION MINDSET: How is your life better because of this intention?

(Get into the right mindset before you continue to write out the EXACT SAME manifestation intention from day 1 below)

1
2
3
4
5
6
7
8
9
10
11
12
13
14
15
16
17
18
19
20
21
22
23
24
25

DAY 4

26

27

28

29

30

31

32

33

34

35

36

37

38

39

40

41

42

43

44

45

46

47

48

49

50

51

52

53

54

55

I RELEASE MY INTENTION WITH GRATITUDE AND LOVE,

MANIFESTATION MINDSET: Why are you grateful to have this intention?

(Get into the right mindset before you continue to write out the EXACT SAME manifestation intention from day 1 below)

1

2

3

4

5

6

7

8

9

10

11

12

13

14

15

16

17

18

19

20

21

22

23

24

25

26

27

28

29

30

31

32

33

34

35

36

37

38

39

40

41

42

43

44

45

46

47

48

49

50

51

52

53

54

55

I RELEASE MY INTENTION WITH GRATITUDE AND LOVE,

55X5 CHALLENGE COMPLETION

55X5 CHALLENGE COMPLETION

MANIFESTATION INTENTION:

(In the present tense & a place of gratitude, write a clear statement of your intended manifestation as if you already have it)

1
2
3
4
5
6
7
8
9
10
11
12
13
14
15
16
17
18
19
20
21
22
23
24
25

26

27

28

29

30

31

32

33

34

35

36

37

38

39

40

41

42

43

44

45

46

47

48

49

50

51

52

53

54

55

I RELEASE MY INTENTION WITH GRATITUDE AND LOVE,

MANIFESTATION MINDSET: Why do you desire this intention in your life?

(Get into the right mindset before you continue to write out the EXACT SAME manifestation intention from day 1 below)

1
2
3
4
5
6
7
8
9
10
11
12
13
14
15
16
17
18
19
20
21
22
23
24
25

26

27

28

29

30

31

32

33

34

35

36

37

38

39

40

41

42

43

44

45

46

47

48

49

50

51

52

53

54

55

I RELEASE MY INTENTION WITH GRATITUDE AND LOVE,

MANIFESTATION MINDSET: Why does this intention excite you?

(Get into the right mindset before you continue to write out the EXACT SAME manifestation intention from day 1 below)

1

2

3

4

5

6

7

8

9

10

11

12

13

14

15

16

17

18

19

20

21

22

23

24

25

26
27
28
29
30
31
32
33
34
35
36
37
38
39
40
41
42
43
44
45
46
47
48
49
50
51
52
53
54
55

I RELEASE MY INTENTION WITH GRATITUDE AND LOVE,

MANIFESTATION MINDSET: How is your life better because of this intention?

(Get into the right mindset before you continue to write out the EXACT SAME manifestation intention from day 1 below)

1
2
3
4
5
6
7
8
9
10
11
12
13
14
15
16
17
18
19
20
21
22
23
24
25

26
27
28
29
30
31
32
33
34
35
36
37
38
39
40
41
42
43
44
45
46
47
48
49
50
51
52
53
54
55

I RELEASE MY INTENTION WITH GRATITUDE AND LOVE,

MANIFESTATION MINDSET: Why are you grateful to have this intention?

(Get into the right mindset before you continue to write out the EXACT SAME manifestation intention from day 1 below)

1

2

3

4

5

6

7

8

9

10

11

12

13

14

15

16

17

18

19

20

21

22

23

24

25

26
27
28
29
30
31
32
33
34
35
36
37
38
39
40
41
42
43
44
45
46
47
48
49
50
51
52
53
54
55

I RELEASE MY INTENTION WITH GRATITUDE AND LOVE,

MANIFESTED INTENTION:

(REWRITE THE EXACT SAME manifestation intention from day 1 above)

MANIFESTATION SUCCESS STORY

Use these pages to write, illustrate or attach photos, receipts, evidence or proof of your 55x5 Success Story. This will help to document your manifesting journey and minimize resistence to future manifestations and the Law of Attraction.

MANIFESTATION INTENTION:

(In the present tense & a place of gratitude, write a clear statement of your intended manifestation as if you already have it)

1
2
3
4
5
6
7
8
9
10
11
12
13
14
15
16
17
18
19
20
21
22
23
24
25

26
27
28
29
30
31
32
33
34
35
36
37
38
39
40
41
42
43
44
45
46
47
48
49
50
51
52
53
54
55

I RELEASE MY INTENTION WITH GRATITUDE AND LOVE,

MANIFESTED INTENTION:

(REWRITE THE EXACT SAME manifestation intention from day 1 above)

MANIFESTATION SUCCESS STORY

Use these pages to write, illustrate or attach photos, receipts, evidence or proof of your 55x5 Success Story. This will help to document your manifesting journey and minimize resistence to future manifestations and the Law of Attraction.

MANIFESTATION MINDSET: Why do you desire this intention in your life?

(Get into the right mindset before you continue to write out the EXACT SAME manifestation intention from day 1 below)

1

2

3

4

5

6

7

8

9

10

11

12

13

14

15

16

17

18

19

20

21

22

23

24

25

26
27
28
29
30
31
32
33
34
35
36
37
38
39
40
41
42
43
44
45
46
47
48
49
50
51
52
53
54
55

I RELEASE MY INTENTION WITH GRATITUDE AND LOVE,

MANIFESTATION MINDSET: Why does this intention excite you?

(Get into the right mindset before you continue to write out the EXACT SAME manifestation intention from day 1 below)

1
2
3
4
5
6
7
8
9
10
11
12
13
14
15
16
17
18
19
20
21
22
23
24
25

26
27
28
29
30
31
32
33
34
35
36
37
38
39
40
41
42
43
44
45
46
47
48
49
50
51
52
53
54
55

I RELEASE MY INTENTION WITH GRATITUDE AND LOVE,

MANIFESTATION MINDSET: How is your life better because of this intention?

(Get into the right mindset before you continue to write out the EXACT SAME manifestation intention from day 1 below)

1
2
3
4
5
6
7
8
9
10
11
12
13
14
15
16
17
18
19
20
21
22
23
24
25

26

27

28

29

30

31

32

33

34

35

36

37

38

39

40

41

42

43

44

45

46

47

48

49

50

51

52

53

54

55

I RELEASE MY INTENTION WITH GRATITUDE AND LOVE,

MANIFESTATION MINDSET: Why are you grateful to have this intention?

(Get into the right mindset before you continue to write out the EXACT SAME manifestation intention from day 1 below)

1
2
3
4
5
6
7
8
9
10
11
12
13
14
15
16
17
18
19
20
21
22
23
24
25

26
27
28
29
30
31
32
33
34
35
36
37
38
39
40
41
42
43
44
45
46
47
48
49
50
51
52
53
54
55

I RELEASE MY INTENTION WITH GRATITUDE AND LOVE,

55X5 CHALLENGE COMPLETED ON DATE _____/_____/_____ TIME _____:_____ AM / PM

MANIFESTED INTENTION:

(REWRITE THE EXACT SAME manifestation intention from day 1 above)

MANIFESTATION SUCCESS STORY

Use these pages to write, illustrate or attach photos, receipts, evidence or proof of your 55x5 Success Story. This will help to document your manifesting journey and minimize resistence to future manifestations and the Law of Attraction.

55X5 CHALLENGE COMPLETION

MANIFESTATION INTENTION:

(In the present tense & a place of gratitude, write a clear statement of your intended manifestation as if you already have it)

1
2
3
4
5
6
7
8
9
10
11
12
13
14
15
16
17
18
19
20
21
22
23
24
25

26
27
28
29
30
31
32
33
34
35
36
37
38
39
40
41
42
43
44
45
46
47
48
49
50
51
52
53
54
55

I RELEASE MY INTENTION WITH GRATITUDE AND LOVE,

MANIFESTATION MINDSET: Why do you desire this intention in your life?

(Get into the right mindset before you continue to write out the EXACT SAME manifestation intention from day 1 below)

1
2
3
4
5
6
7
8
9
10
11
12
13
14
15
16
17
18
19
20
21
22
23
24
25

26
27
28
29
30
31
32
33
34
35
36
37
38
39
40
41
42
43
44
45
46
47
48
49
50
51
52
53
54
55

I RELEASE MY INTENTION WITH GRATITUDE AND LOVE,

MANIFESTATION MINDSET: Why does this intention excite you?

(Get into the right mindset before you continue to write out the EXACT SAME manifestation intention from day 1 below)

1
2
3
4
5
6
7
8
9
10
11
12
13
14
15
16
17
18
19
20
21
22
23
24
25

26
27
28
29
30
31
32
33
34
35
36
37
38
39
40
41
42
43
44
45
46
47
48
49
50
51
52
53
54
55

I RELEASE MY INTENTION WITH GRATITUDE AND LOVE,

MANIFESTATION MINDSET: How is your life better because of this intention?

(Get into the right mindset before you continue to write out the EXACT SAME manifestation intention from day 1 below)

1
2
3
4
5
6
7
8
9
10
11
12
13
14
15
16
17
18
19
20
21
22
23
24
25

26
27
28
29
30
31
32
33
34
35
36
37
38
39
40
41
42
43
44
45
46
47
48
49
50
51
52
53
54
55

I RELEASE MY INTENTION WITH GRATITUDE AND LOVE,

MANIFESTATION MINDSET: Why are you grateful to have this intention?

(Get into the right mindset before you continue to write out the EXACT SAME manifestation intention from day 1 below)

1

2

3

4

5

6

7

8

9

10

11

12

13

14

15

16

17

18

19

20

21

22

23

24

25

26

27

28

29

30

31

32

33

34

35

36

37

38

39

40

41

42

43

44

45

46

47

48

49

50

51

52

53

54

55

I RELEASE MY INTENTION WITH GRATITUDE AND LOVE,

55X5 CHALLENGE COMPLETED ON DATE _____/_____/_____ TIME _____:_____ AM / PM

MANIFESTED INTENTION:

(REWRITE THE EXACT SAME manifestation intention from day 1 above)

MANIFESTATION SUCCESS STORY

Use these pages to write, illustrate or attach photos, receipts, evidence or proof of your 55x5 Success Story. This will help to document your manifesting journey and minimize resistence to future manifestations and the Law of Attraction.

55X5 CHALLENGE COMPLETION

MANIFESTATION INTENTION:

(In the present tense & a place of gratitude, write a clear statement of your intended manifestation as if you already have it)

1
2
3
4
5
6
7
8
9
10
11
12
13
14
15
16
17
18
19
20
21
22
23
24
25

26
27
28
29
30
31
32
33
34
35
36
37
38
39
40
41
42
43
44
45
46
47
48
49
50
51
52
53
54
55

I RELEASE MY INTENTION WITH GRATITUDE AND LOVE,

MANIFESTATION MINDSET: Why do you desire this intention in your life?

(Get into the right mindset before you continue to write out the EXACT SAME manifestation intention from day 1 below)

1

2

3

4

5

6

7

8

9

10

11

12

13

14

15

16

17

18

19

20

21

22

23

24

25

DAY 2

26
27
28
29
30
31
32
33
34
35
36
37
38
39
40
41
42
43
44
45
46
47
48
49
50
51
52
53
54
55

I RELEASE MY INTENTION WITH GRATITUDE AND LOVE,

MANIFESTATION MINDSET: Why does this intention excite you?

(Get into the right mindset before you continue to write out the EXACT SAME manifestation intention from day 1 below)

1
2
3
4
5
6
7
8
9
10
11
12
13
14
15
16
17
18
19
20
21
22
23
24
25

26

27

28

29

30

31

32

33

34

35

36

37

38

39

40

41

42

43

44

45

46

47

48

49

50

51

52

53

54

55

I RELEASE MY INTENTION WITH GRATITUDE AND LOVE,

MANIFESTATION MINDSET: How is your life better because of this intention?

(Get into the right mindset before you continue to write out the EXACT SAME manifestation intention from day 1 below)

1
2
3
4
5
6
7
8
9
10
11
12
13
14
15
16
17
18
19
20
21
22
23
24
25

26

27

28

29

30

31

32

33

34

35

36

37

38

39

40

41

42

43

44

45

46

47

48

49

50

51

52

53

54

55

I RELEASE MY INTENTION WITH GRATITUDE AND LOVE,

MANIFESTATION MINDSET: Why are you grateful to have this intention?

(Get into the right mindset before you continue to write out the EXACT SAME manifestation intention from day 1 below)

1
2
3
4
5
6
7
8
9
10
11
12
13
14
15
16
17
18
19
20
21
22
23
24
25

DAY 5

26
27
28
29
30
31
32
33
34
35
36
37
38
39
40
41
42
43
44
45
46
47
48
49
50
51
52
53
54
55

I RELEASE MY INTENTION WITH GRATITUDE AND LOVE,

MANIFESTED INTENTION:

(REWRITE THE EXACT SAME manifestation intention from day 1 above)

MANIFESTATION SUCCESS STORY

Use these pages to write, illustrate or attach photos, receipts, evidence or proof of your 55x5 Success Story. This will help to document your manifesting journey and minimize resistence to future manifestations and the Law of Attraction.

55X5 CHALLENGE COMPLETION

Made in the USA
Las Vegas, NV
18 November 2024

12083232R00065